# ԹՎԵՐԻ ՊԱՏՄՈՒԹՅՈՒՆԸ

## THE NUMBER STORY

### SMALL BOOK ONE

#### ENGLISH – EASTERN ARMENIAN

*Numbers Teach Children*
*Their Number Names*

written and illustrated by

# MISS ANNA

Early Reader Edition of *The Number Story 1*
Bronze Medal Winner, 2016 Wishing Shelf Book Award

Library of Congress Control Number: 2018902040

Names: Miss Anna, author.
Title: Number story : numbers teach children their number names / Miss Anna.
Description: Portland, OR: Lumpy Publishing, 2018.
Identifiers: ISBN 978-1-945977-87-9 | LCCN 2018902040
Summary: The pictures and rhymes present stories which introduce numbers 0-10.
Subjects: LCSH Numeration—English--Armenian--Pictorial works--Juvenile literature. | BISAC JUVENILE NONFICTION /
Languages: English--Armenian
Classification: LCC QA141.3 .M57 2018 | DDC 513—dc23

Publisher: Lumpy Publishing
Website: www.missannabooks.com
Email: missanna@missannabooks.com

Paperback: ISBN 978-1-945977-87-9
Printed in the U.S.A.    1 3 5 7 9 10 8 6 4 2

Կուզե՞ք սովորել թվերի անունները:

It is very easy and a lot of fun!

Շատ հեշտ է և շա՛տ հետաքրքիր:

Say-along our little jingle

Մեզ հետ երգե՛ք մեր փոքր երգը:

starting from Number One!

Եկե՛ք սկսենք մեկից:

# 1

## Մեկ

Մեկը նման է իմ մի մատին:

ONE!

Մէ՛կ:

# 2

TWO trails a tail.

ԵՐԿՈՒ

Երկուն պոչ ունի:

A TAIL! ጣጠ Ձ:

# 3

THREE   has bumps.

ԵՐԵՔ

Երեքը ունի բլուրներ:

Նայե՛ք կանաչ բլուրներին:

# 4

**FOUR** carries a sail.

ՉՈՐՍ

Չորսն առագաստ է կրում:

A SAIL!
ԱՌԱԳԱ՛ՍՏ:
Նավը առագաստո՛վ է:

# 5

FIVE   is a racing track.

Հ Ի Ն Գ

Հինգը մրցատաշտ է:

VROOM
Վռումմ:

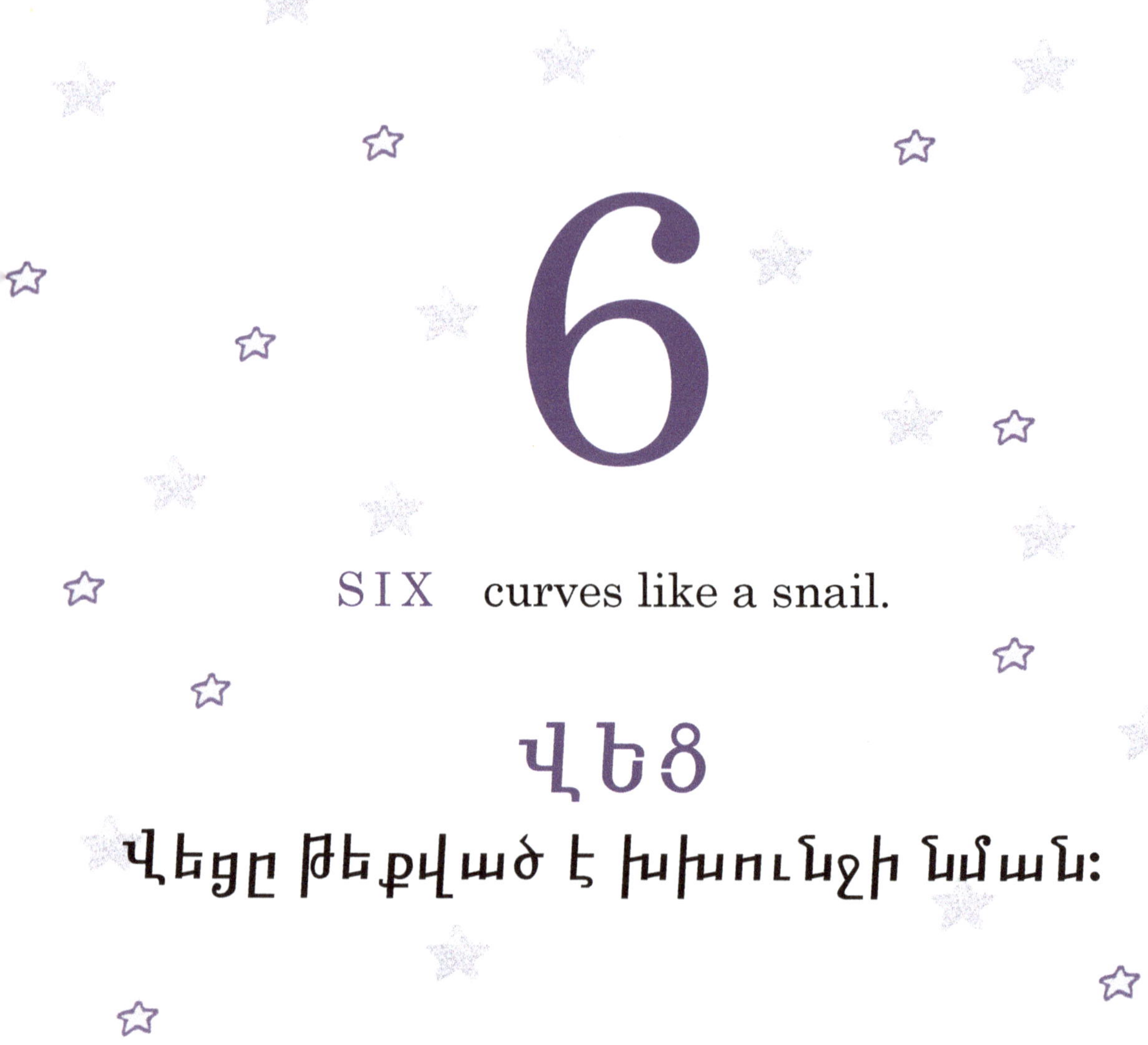

# 6

S I X   curves like a snail.

## ՎԵՑ

Վեցը թեքված է խխունջի նման:

A SNAIL!   ԽԽՈՒ ԻՆՉ:

7
SEVEN has a sharp angle.
ՅՈԹ
Յոթն ունի սուր անկյուն:

BE CAREFUL! IT'S SHARP!
Զգո՛յշ եղէք: Սո՛ւր է:

# 8

ՈՒՌԱ՛:
YIPPEE!

NINE   is a bubble on a stick.

ԻՆԸ

Ինը փուչիկ է փայտի վրա:

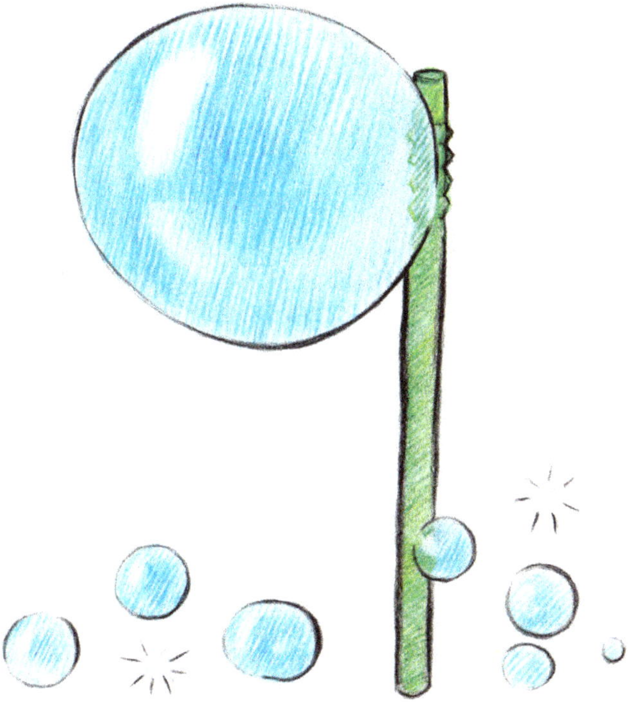

A BUBBLE! ՊՂՊՋԱ՜Կ։

# 10

TEN   is an eye of a whale.

ՏԱՍԸ

Տասը կետի աչքն է:

HELLO!
ԲԱՐԵՒ:

And

ԵՎ

O

ZERO   is an empty pail.

ԶՐՈ

Զրոն դատարկ դույլ է:

IT'S
EMPTY!
Դատարկ է:

Thank you for playing with us today.

We had a lot of fun too!

Շնորհակալություն մեզ հետ
այսօր խաղալու համար։

Մենք շատ լավ ժամանակ ենք անցկացրել։

We are your Number friends,
Zero to Ten,
Who will be here for you~
Մենք ձեր թվային ընկերներն ենք:
Մենք միշտ ձեզ հետ կլինենք:


Bye-bye now!
See you again soon!
Ցտեսությո՛ւն:
Նորից կտեսնվենք՝ շատ շուտով:

The Numbers are *SINGING* too!

To sing-a-long, look for Miss Anna Number Story
at your favorite music store like iTUNES.

MP3

| Numbers 0-10<br>IDENTIFYING<br>& COUNTING | Numbers 11-20<br>& Ordinals<br><br>first, second, third... | Numbers 0-100<br>& Place Values<br><br>ones, tens, hundreds... | About Clocks<br>& Telling Time<br><br>hours, minutes, seconds |

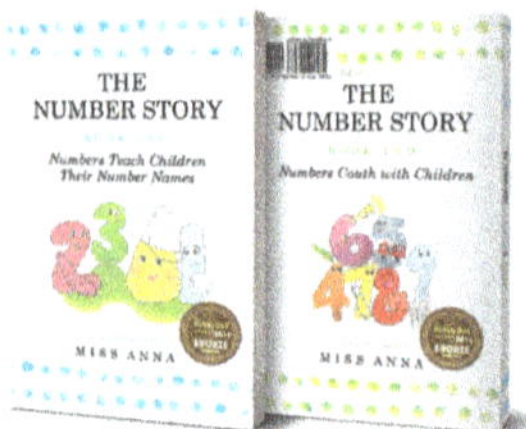   

| Number Story 1 & 2 | Number Story 3 & 4 | Number Story 5 & 6 | Number Story 7 & 8 |
| isbn: 978-0-996216-48-7 | isbn: 978-1-945977-01-5 | isbn: 978-1-945977-06-0 | isbn: 978-1-949320-40-4 |

For more Miss Anna books to love,
visit us at

www.missannabooks.com

Numbers are working hard all over the world!
*Come Travel the World with Us!*